DROWNED:

A MERMAID'S MANIFESTO

THERESA DAVIS

SIBLING RIVALRY PRESS
LITTLE ROCK, ARKANSAS
DISTURB / ENRAPTURE

Drowned: A Mermaid's Manifesto
Copyright © 2016 by Theresa Davis

Cover art by Cindy Taylor
Author photograph by K. Moment Photography
kmomentproductions.wix.com/photography
Cover design by Seth Pennington and Bryan Borland

Sibling Rivalry Press, LLC
PO Box 26147
Little Rock, AR 72221

info@siblingrivalrypress.com

www.siblingrivalrypress.com

ISBN: 978-1-943977-23-9

Library of Congress Control No. 2016945235

This title is housed permanently in the Rare Books and Special Collections Vault of the Library of Congress.

First Sibling Rivalry Press Edition, September 2016

To my mother Alice Lovelace, the Mermaid of all Mermaids.

For my family, especially my children, who inspire me to be my authentic self.

To all the strong women whose support is a bright light, a call to action, or a shot of tequila in a smoky bar.

I am forever grateful.

Contents

I *had a dream one night.*

In the dream I was being lectured by Frida Kahlo, Medusa, and Eve. These are my muses. They make frequent visits, and I am lucky or unlucky enough to have total recall of my dreams. This night in particular I had a lot on my mind. The morning started with the shooting of another unarmed young black man. Men were telling me what to do with my body and threatening laws. A white man shot a lot of people, was arrested, and given a bulletproof vest for his safety.

Medusa was riled up and would not give any of the other sisters room for their words. She had a point to make and wanted no interruptions until it was made. She explained that the anxiety I was feeling was normal. "Who better than me," she said, "to recognize when people and things are actually trying to kill you? Not with swords and shit like they used when they came for me, but like literally and metaphorically *this world is trying to kill you.* A black woman with children and an opinion and a voice that people listen to. Mentally and emotionally trying to take you out. You must think things that no one who is *not* like you ever has to think about. Bulletproof vest, my ass!"

She roamed the room waving her arms, her hair hissing in her wake. She had our full attention, and soon she had us nodding in agreement. She threw post-it notes at our heads, and we were instructed to make notes of all the attacks on women and their bodies and their brains and their humanity we could think of. The bar's wall—the dream always happens in a bar... don't ask me why... okay, I know why—anyway, the walls were full of little post-it notes with our words on them. We stood back and looked at our great and good work. Eve, who is always wearing something short and tight "to prove a point," she always says, allowed a smile to take over her face. She said, "I always wanted to have a Manifesto! Something that says, *Look! This is what I am, and you will not make me what I am not!*"

We group-hugged looking at our wall of things that try to kill us in different ways every single day. In my dreams, fictional, imagined or not, Frida, Medusa, and Eve are real and here and connected, probably because they are in my head, and I am real and connected. (Just stay with me here.)

Frida ordered a round of shots, tequila if you must know, and proposed a toast. "They try to drown us," she started, and I thought for sure she was going to recite one of my favorite quotes, then she flipped the script. "But little do those fuckers know we are Mermaids! You can't drown a Mermaid!" We toasted, tapped our shots on the bar, drank, and slammed the glasses down so hard they shattered.

I woke up, and *Drowned: A Mermaid's Manifesto* was on the tip of my tongue. I worried over this book for months. I worried that my anger was all over the place, and I did not want to be perceived as ANGRY BLACK WOMAN.

Then, I was like, wait, I *am* angry, in different places about different things, and I write poems about my feelings because *I am a poet*. My anger comes from real places, and I am sure others feel as I feel, and these poems are for them. Or maybe, instead of people asking me to educate them on the issues that challenge me as a woman, as a black woman, as a black woman who is a mother, as a black woman who is a mother and also as gay as the day is long, they will read these poems and educate themselves.

I am surrounded by women who make me want to move and disrupt and change things all the time, fully aware that not everyone has this life or the kind of support that I have. I take none of the women in my life for granted and consider this a celebration of all the Mermaids in my life. I am grateful for all my muses living, dead, and the rowdy ones that show up in smoky bars in my dreams. Who remind me daily through their strength and perseverance that it is so very true: you cannot drown a Mermaid!

I drank to drown my sorrows,
but the damned things learned how to swim.

- Frida Kahlo -

Manifesto

there are things that will not be disputed

or argued away
or touched with hands
that claw or pull
or assumed out or into me

this body
the dark brown black of it
the tooth and nail of it
the five decades strong in it
the broken, healed, and ripped at the core of it
the stutter in my stumble
this exploding heart
getting my love on everything
this loaded litany of my mouth
the same mouth that punishes
the same mouth that pleasures
the mouth taken out of context
the mouth refusing further colonization
of her voice
her story
her truth

the one taking it all back

this is the part where you try to fill in my blanks
with
you're so articulate for a black woman
so strong for a black woman
so pretty for a black woman
as if my power
my beauty
my articulation

does not exist unless you say it does

I will not let you claim
this all of me
this is the language of my body
full of everything
including the fear and anger of it

because it is always there
just under the surface

I stay on top of it

this is how I do not drown

B*lack*

a noose of night
pits and ditch water
vacant eyes full of questions
backbone and background to the blues
flashing lights
positions assumed
a gun the shape of a wallet
the shape of a bachelor party
the shape of a twelve-year-old boy
open carry and stand your ground
a split of lightning
leather and shine
staring into the void
a place to hide your voice
hands raised in surrender
backs full of bullets
a jolt of caffeine
ink spreading a stain
a bruise of words
pot and kettle
the space between the blinks
texas tea
bodies outlined in chalk

A^{drift}

when your anchor loses purchase
drags you back to a past of famine
of confusion
disturbing the vultures
at the bottom of your ocean
you doubt gravity

question if anything holds you to this earth
when all around you is letting go
if you open your fist
will you float
or sink this beautiful ship dream
crafted to the tune of your forgetting

when she stops talking
you accuse yourself of faulty communication
ignore the morse code reporting rip tides
in a sea you thought you knew

you spy the compass
see if you are still pointing north
still on the right trajectory
to strike the stars

when your anchor is suddenly gone
even when suddenly happens in slow motion
you become floating hazard
wings clipped by an unforgiving sun

You think I made this happen

you are wrong
you just don't know it yet

trying to fix what you did not break
remembering all the distractions
the smoke, most of the mirrors

you reflected a truth she never wanted to see
her need for familiar neglect
you were too much ocean to keep her
the sky opens up
the rains come

with new sea legs
you navigate different
mark the spot to remember
where you never want to be again
sink your hand into your chest
remove the part that feels
you never want to feel this again
change your course
sail for calmer seas

vow to stop semaphoring a love
that will never love you back
lock down all that wasted emotion
turned siren song
turned show tune

later you will laugh
but now the salt stings
you become an island for eighteen months
moored in reliving the event
convinced your ship was never worthy

Receptacle

when she opened her mouth
the rains came
the moon had a song to share

no one recognized
her hollowed-out voice
no one heard
the scuff of disinterested shoes

a day of mourning
after morning comes
hope packed her bags

left

arms shaky from resisting
from trying to hold up
a sky in the perpetual act of falling

the misery of holding your breath
and your empty palms full of threats

they ask for proof of life
of existence
of existing
then only offer bullets
wrapped in brown skin
a song we have heard before
lyrics we know so well

the fact of rain
never rules out drought
or drowning

while
standing on your feet
minding your own business
hands raised slightly
above your head
chest exposed
you pray for rain

without the lightning
without the thunder

Compunction

her mouth full of hands
tries to hold what she cannot taste
truth or those pretending to be

cannot smell the memories
the staccato screams stuck between her toes
feels the beat beneath her feet
a tilting earth shallow, sweet and sour

her hair drags the floor
collecting the dust of what is left
names each regret
hangs them around her head

holding court with spilled tongues
and pregnant pauses
skin sallow and sunken
the dull of her treasure
forecasts her coming apart

oh, shiny piñata Mermaid girl
trying to walk on land
trying to drown her ocean
in some shape she has never been

heart bruised and hungry
everything but sweet strikes the ground
the confection tune of
a song she thinks remembers

only the words

the melody
lost

Home

I lie to myself far too often
unspoken
a lie all the same
shielding others
a habit I've held too close
a lover I never wanted
lips singed from flashbacks

this park owns a block
I stop only because there is a pond
shallow yet deep enough to drown
the words under my breath
I will lay down these burdens
confess all to myself
cool my hands in the moving water
a baptism

there are children here who know I do not belong
seem to understand that this body poses no danger
not to them, maybe to herself
receiving pity from the eyes of children
has a restorative power
they see more than we care to know

soon they will forget my sadness
distracted by the turtles
their carapace absorbing all the sun
one day in the future they might remember me
the land bound Mermaid, the way she
stared unblinking at the water's surface

the children will wonder if
I too admired the turtles
or was I lost
just trying to find my way home

T*en*

remembering your body
the fold and soft of it
the curve of your lines
all strength and beauty
a breath caught on moonlight's magic

the way we contrast with our
complementary colors
the sweet slice of your mouth
the way you say what you
want me to do to you
in my ear
on my skin
bringing out the gentleman in me

a new spin on this adventure
unplanned

maybe

newly remodeled
standing the test of old times
understanding familiar rhythms
never missing a beat
the hot and swoon of it
stuck in my throat
quicksilver fingers
hips dancing on my tongue
remembering the geography of you
move and friction
the way you look at me

the way I drown in the scent of you
the way you still make me blush
all over

Phillumenist
(n) a collector of matchbooks and matchboxes

When the men came. They glued their eyes to my skin
and never forgot my hue. The way their sockets jittered
I could tell they were afraid. I could not understand why
brown has always been my favorite color.

The sun was bright that day. The sun has always
loved the tickle on my skin. The men wore no skin.
They only wore eyes. They only wore eyes for me.

The way they stared. The more they stared I learned what
fear smelled like. It was the scent of brown skin baking
under a bright so delicious they longed to possess
or destroy the object of their affection. Eyes focused on my skin.

I dreamed that night. In the dream, the moon was full.
That night in the dream the men came wearing masks
camouflaging their fear. Their pointy hats aimed at the moon,
their eyes still glued to my skin.

They made the most unnatural sounds. Their teeth splintered
wood. They shouted all of their words. I did not speak
their language, did not understand their shade of hate.
They waved their arms but would not let me leave.

Then one man struck a match. He laid it next to my skin
and watched me drown in flames.

I burned all night.

D^{uctile}

you are not soft

you are hard

she says this
fingers twisted in my dread
pressing on the protrusion
between my thighs
says she must have imagined my tears
because I do not come off
as a girl who wears them
the moment goes by so fast

she says she loves the feel of me
solid
a wall pushing against her curves
I show her my soft spots
she cringes
calls me a liar wrapped in a kiss

I remove the apparatus
create the distance needed
to breathe her goodbye
pretend to not be tender
drown my feelings in concrete

when she leaves
I shower to the point of boil
try to wash the stain of her away
strap on my armor once again
reupholster my smile
leave all my soft in the towel
slung over the sink

if I see her again
I will be a wall she cannot climb
a door that she can only enter
when I can no longer bare my soft

Hypocrisy Suite Movement #1
Sanctimony in G Minor

Once a week
she drags her bones from her bed,
decorates her body,
her temple of hope and everlasting joy.

She eats bread made with her own hands
full of love and thanksgiving,
a prayer over every bite.

Bible tucked neatly in purse,
she walks head held high and mighty
into her church of God.

There she will praise, sing songs full of shouts,
and amen. She will dance for her deity, all jumps
and waving arms. Thanking God for the love in her heart,
the love she has for mankind,
tambourines chiming in the distance.

Tomorrow she will show her real face.

Tomorrow she will walk into my church.

Tomorrow she will hear me preach my truth.

Tomorrow she will call me faggot
in a whisper that carries.

She will sandwich the slur in her cheek
between her prayers and hallelujahs.

Congenial

when I was with you
I was not me
just something to do
on a random Wednesday
puckered and withdrawn
an overdue library book
faded
neglected on the shelf
of your intentions

there is no room for regret in my heart
I loved you the only way I knew how
drowned myself under your feet
you could not help yourself
I was so handy that year

and you wore expensive shoes

what other use is there
for a willing device

M*ermaid*

then there are days when the waves overtake me
usually in the mornings when the stucco ceiling writhes
an ocean over my head the covers become so heavy
I cannot free myself from the undertow of memories
all this sand in my hair in my bed

I rise anyway because that is what you do when you have
mouths to feed and you have these legs you wanted
so desperately, you traded them for silence

B*asa*

The woman on the bus got knocked around,
beaten down, raped and bound.

While the driver of the bus complicit
and strange drove the rapist around
so they could play their rape games.

As he picked up more passengers who
pretended not to notice the two-hour attack
and the woman left hopeless.

Through the sounds and the screams
of flesh being ripped or six men
who decided that pain they'd inflict.

And the wheels on this bus they just
travel around and no one hears a sound
as it goes all through town.

Does this bus that hates women
as it moves, as it probes, only stalk
roads in India or does it travel the globe?

Because it leaves me a shadow, makes
me wonder if they'd see if that woman was you
or that woman was me.

Because that woman on the bus got knocked around,
beaten down, raped and bound.

While the driver of the bus just drove around.
All
through
the
town.

A*mnesia*

there was that year
I forgot the sound of my name
I remember it began
with the sound of tongue
pressed to teeth ended
with the sound of relief

that same year
I became somebody's wife
somebody else's mother

I did not know myself
but answered every time
I heard that name
that thunder clap
that drowning deluge
that me
I used to be

H ypocrisy Suite Movement #2
Tithes in A Minor

for my sperm donor

36 Years Ago

Today,
I will ask if I can go to the movies with a boy I like.

Today,
you will insist that I go to Planned Parenthood,
self-medicate my need to lose my virginity.

When I explain that it is just a movie with a friend,
that I am not interested in sex,
you will quote Corinthians 6:18;

Flee from sexual immorality. Every sin a person commits
is outside the body, but the sexually immoral person sins
against his own body.

You will lecture me about temptation.
You will remind me about Eve.

When I mention that it was Adam who actually broke the rule
you will call me blasphemous, demand I get saved, repent.

Tomorrow,
you and your former mistress-turned-wife will watch
porn until you orgasm.
Punish me for overhearing.
Remind me of my sinner ways.

At church,
you will force me to talk to the pastor.

I will tell him everything you think I am not brave
enough to say.

I will ask,

Pastor, Who are the sinners here?

He will not answer.
I will not question his bravery but I make sure
we have an understanding.
I smirk,
just a little, as the pastor's sermon speaks of giving
in to the flesh.
Congratulate myself for being his inspiration.

Get a little sick
when you and the woman you cheated on my
mother with *Amen* in harmony.

I'll catch the pastor's eye, mouth the word *hypocrite*,
as your former mistress catches the Holy Spirit.

In her holy dance,
she makes the same sounds she makes during
orgasm.

I wonder if her God approves
of all the ways she comes.

How to Escape from Killer Bees

if they begin flying around you
if they begin to sting you
do not run away
do not SWAT their attempts
it only makes them angrier
it only makes the triggers pull faster
no shelter will give you cover
if your skin is dark
they will be more attracted
they will offer you no escape
kicked in doors
hands round necks
gunshot residue perfuming your skin
the venom will continue
to pump into your body
400-plus years
even if you jump into water
no fan tied to your throat
no money in your pockets
no whistle leaking from your lips
they are likely to be waiting
when you surface
sTILL

On Loving You

then there was the time
I let lonely drag me back to your bed
this time for the last time

I meant it

I still do

every single time

Fabular
adj; to tell a story exaggerating in the form of a fable

The way I saw it, she walked right in.
No, she didn't walk,
she kind of sauntered, maybe a swagger
rolling her hips in that way.

Or maybe she strolled, like she could care less,
but you could tell she cared a lot.

Anyway, she walked, sauntered, strolled in
like she owned that place, or at the very
least her space in that place.

I swear I ain't never seen nobody enter a room
the ways she did, not a care in the world, her rolling hips.

Then she stood perfectly still.

Okay maybe she moved, just a little.
But she was perfectly still in that way
you knew something was going to happen,
and it might be scary but you wanted to see.

She stood perfectly still,
kinda, and looked at everybody like
they owed her money and best be ready to pay up.

Then she made eye contact with this woman.
She was a beautiful woman the way she blushed
when their eyes locked.
She only blushed in her eyes when that woman
looked at her
the way she did.

Then she did that walk again, all saunter, swagger, stroll
and rolling hips.
She walked right up to that beautiful woman and smiled.
Showing no teeth, but we saw them all.

It was like they knew each other, but not really,
you could tell.
I mean there was chemistry, it was everywhere,
it kinda bounced around the room.
They didn't notice and we didn't mind.
It got on everybody and the walls.
Then she, the woman, plunged her hand into her chest.
Just stuck it in there, her hand in her chest.
She reached inside her chest and it was magical.
Her hand disappeared inside and she just pulled it out.
Pulled it right out.
She just pulled her heart right out of her chest
and handed it,
her heart, to the beautiful woman like, like it was normal.

Like people just walk, saunter, swagger, stroll,
hips rolling,
not a care in the world,
perfectly still,
but moving,
all smile no teeth,
eye contact and chemistry bouncing around the room,
plunging their hand in their chest
pulling out their heart and
handing it to a beautiful woman,
like people do that every day.
Like magic.
Like normal.

Then she said three words.
She just said three words.

She looked at that beautiful woman, smiling,
showing no teeth and said,

This is yours.

She said it just like that,

This is yours.

Only three words and her heart.
She just handed it, her heart and three words to a
beautiful woman.

The beautiful woman smiled,
blushing in her eyes, she smiled and simply said,

Thank you.

She said it just like that
holding that heart in her hand.
She tucked it inside of her own heart.

I tell you, I ain't never seen no shit like that before.

Copse
(n). a small wood

The floor said,

"Did you know that I used to be a tree
upright touching the sky
swaying to the beat of breezes?

Until the men came,
with their weapons of destruction.
They cut me down in my prime.

They took away my roots.
They took my stretching arms.
Took my skin.
Made me a dead, flat thing.

When they drove the metal through my flesh,
I found
I could still feel.
I feel it every time they walk across my face.
I felt you
Brown Girl,
the way you took off your shoes
before stepping lightly across my body,
an act so full of respect
I thought, no,
I knew you would listen.
Knew you would hear what others can or will not.

I saw your brother once, Brown Girl.
He stood tall and proud.
Until the man came
with an ax the likes
I'd never seen before.
He aimed it at your brother.

Drove metal through his exploding flesh.
Cut him down.
There was so much blood.

I had a brother too, Brown Girl.
He stood right next to me.
We two stood tall and proud and wild and family.
Then the men.
They bent his flesh
made him box,
placed your brother inside.

When they bury your brother
inside of mine,
a brown seed
in the brown earth,
Girl, what will he grow into?

I hope not a tree.

Not to live the same death twice.

They have planted so many of you,

an entire forest."

Hypocrisy Suite Movement #3
The Parade in F Major

You and your complicated mouth,
drinking whiskey, shooting up the room.
We have become something and nothing
simultaneously,
absorbed in thought between moments
of mutual distractions.

A reenactment,
a pause,
an accidental backtrack in the sidewalk.
Concrete growing beneath our feet.
A lie in the pulpit.

Your hug, an uncomfortable chair,
shapes me awkwardly.

I have drowned in your shallow.

I have become a well-timed spit after a blow job.
You want all the space in the room.

I comply, show you my retreating back,
my slow migration to somewhere else,
but I think I love you
with this ticker-tape heart,
all float no real direction.

F*lotsam*

and when she could no longer
float on her back
she turned over
spread her arms wide

she opened her too big mouth
took a deep breath
watched herself float out to sea

Two Figures with Flowers

I am two states away staring at the same picture
that hangs on a wall in your house. It reminds me
of the last time I saw you, flames in the background.

I am staring at this image remembering how tired
I felt in that moment when you shifted into shallow,
all my limbs aching from confinement, my heart
on the floor, torn between relief, craving
the freedom from closeted love
and the grief of losing you.

Two states away my hands, my hips remember the feel
of lust in the dark, away from prying eyes,
a secret I could not keep, not for long,
your body's press on me the way
I reveled and moaned.

Tomorrow I will leave this state, a steering wheel trapped
between my fists headed back to my life, the one you
never inhabited fully.

Is it coincidence that this painting exists
in two different states?
Is it coincidence that you attempted
to siren-song me back
into your bed of lies or that my hands still ache
for the geography of you?

I have been looking for home in all the wrong closets,
in all the wrong smiles, welcomed
more warmly by strangers
than by those who claimed to know me or want to.

This painting, these two figures peer out
so full of sadness.
I feel they may be warning me.
The smaller figure implores,
her hands a fist of flowers.
She wears eyes that seem to say

Do not forget.
Remember what happened last time.

Still Life with Scissors

forgetting you is not working
your face shows up in my morning coffee
cup after cup I suffer in silence with my
memories these shaking hands

your shadow
etched itself on my ceiling
it looms some nights discrediting
my new lovers
mocking their steaming skin
your name tattooed on my tongue
confusing my orgasms

but I can move away from you

for a time

if there be ocean and sand
jellyfish and tide
where you be far off in the distance
an island I cannot travel to
me standing on the shore
waving goodbye to this war between us

I can move away from you
when the salt stings my skin
when I remember my gills my scales
when I release the weight of you

yeah
I can forget your ass at the ocean

but in rush hour traffic
you return road rage

a balled fist anchored
in the roof of my mouth
an articulated fuck you
leaping from my throat
eyes everywhere at once
looking for an exit
a way to stop your lies from changing lanes
to the tune of your mood
no signals
just acceleration

and all the things I loved about you
I still love
so it makes me question
if I even know what love means

I mean

is it love when someone accordions you
into every success they have never had

is it love
if you can only love me in secret
or behind closet doors

is it love when you make me feel so clean
yet so filthy between blinks

Block Party

I have a habit of saving
jumping on my white horse
riding to the rescue
no thought of personal safety
just do the right thing by any means necessary

but the climate of the world today
the way the winds blow these days
cause me to hesitate this time

personal safety a real concern
this time the moment changes me
not in a good way

my neighbors party too hard
too often
their celebratory encounters end
with shouting or violence
usually the men
this time a woman's voice shrill
stills my blood
makes me instinctively reach for my phone
9-1-1 on speed dial

but instead
I stop finger hovering over a screen
ashamed
I take personal stock instead of acting

my neighbors are white
I am not
I could not see how I would not be directly involved

so I wake my roommate

she is white
I drag her to our porch safe haven
ask her to listen
if I should call
she shakes sleep long enough
to register the sounds of need
throws me a nod

I call

then tell her that she has to stay
when they come they will come for me first
she doubts that
the cries coming from across the street
assuring her
she is right
but she stays

five police cars later
four sets of officers head towards the screams
the other set approaches me

I say before they reach my home

the trouble is over there

they ignore my black face
again I say

the trouble is over there

they keep advancing

my roommate stands
shows her white face
the officers stop
nod the way she nodded at me

they head towards the trouble

I have tried to explain what it means to be me
black and trying to do the right thing
how often the one who calls is the one
outlined in chalk

her face museum worthy
registers a myriad of emotions
while I am torn between relief and pissed
that I did not get to ride in on my white horse
but my white roommate rode in on my fear
saved me from danger that should
have never been mine

we both watch transfixed
the drunk and disorderly
are allowed to mount their steed
drive away

watch again as they return minutes later
police sirens and lights following them

watch the white girl I tried to save
exit her vehicle
storm up to the officer
her fingers pointing
her slurred voice raised

at no time does the officer take a defensive stance
at no time do the police feel in danger

she never had the lesson
of what not to do when dealing with police
how she wears her pretty white girl privilege like kevlar

knowing had that been me
had I acted in that way
the chance of someone telling my mother
I am sorry for your loss
could have been my future
how I would not even **GARNER** a hashtag
there would be no march
no riot for this black woman

my roommate's eyes hold mine
her eyes full of tears
my eyes full of rage
both of us fully aware in this moment
what justice does not look like

the drunk girl revs her engine
drives away
the officers look my way
they do not approach
because nothing happened
twice

move along folks
I imagine they are saying
there is nothing to see here

Date Race

when we met that time
I am pretty sure you saw my skin first
deemed it exotic
as in who is that beautiful black woman
who is that potential

you said
I have never been with a black woman
cherry popped
not my issue on either side
I enjoy women the skin they are wrapped in
does not dictate my desire

I fell into the flirting
all abandoned lust
fucked you in the first hour we met
your underwear in my driveway
it should have been one night
a chance encounter
a fuck at the bar

but in the frenzy
we must have exchanged
more than fluids
you had my name and number
so much for casual sex
when we talked you said something clever
enough to mistake gift of gab for intellect
I do enjoy good conversation

ten months later
your dogs have eaten the crotch
out of five pieces of my underwear

the conversation starts to falter
crack in the facade
you call a client a slur
laugh it off but I cannot

How could you be a racist you defend

I am with you aren't I

in the wake of my tirade
you are so beside yourself
drink until you pass out
I let the underwear-eating dogs out to pee
cover your lying frame
and play the words
I am with you aren't I
to a 40-mile soundtrack
the phrase playing over and over
ruining my favorite songs
knowing what it meant
not wanting to see

wondering how many times
you threw that slur around with your friends
laughing off your ability to be racist
because you had a black girlfriend

Hypocrisy Suite Movement #4
Projectile in A Flat

So many things fall from the sky
never to be found again: swallowed whole.

Tragedy never comes in the form we predict.
Sometimes it takes the form of dropped calls
falling from some other time
like nightmares wanting operator assistance
for their return.

Like lips sutured shut after the lie fell,
collateral damage after the rolling stop.

All the signs pointed to this,
warned of pending doom,
this wandering heart ignored.

Now discarded,
this body understands
the danger of whiskey
in the mouth
of a complicated girl
who staggers into hearts,
smashes up the chambers,
quietly loads the gun
tucked in her cheeks.

She aims.
She pulls the trigger.

At Rest Bitch Face

so like Michelle Obama,
my at rest face apparently says fuck you

says back the fuck off
what the fuck do you want
what are you talking about and why the fuck
are you talking to me

I can't actually see my face
so I don't know if this is true
but this is what people have told me
while suggesting

you should smile more and well you need to practice
a better at rest face

I'm not practicing that shit or smiling for your comfort
but I do make a conscious effort
to change it
so now my face says needy hurt forlorn
so people greet me with that face
you know that face
that

poor darling, what in the world, and *bless your heart*

and we who speak southern hear the patronizing in that

or the serious inquiries of

what's the matter are you ok what do you need

which confuses me because nothing's the matter and
I feel fine so my face changes

and now we are back to my original at rest face
which apparently is still saying fuck you

as if the set of my brow furrowed says I'm pissed
and a breath away from flipping tables
or hold my rings while I open this can of whoop…
as if I couldn't just be pondering my next move
or thinking about this idea I've got
it's going to be amazing
look at this furrowed brow
look how hard I've been thinking
why can't I just be thinking
why I gotta be all pissed and what the fuck

and I wonder for a moment if it's because I'm black
and you expect all black women to be angry
so full of it that it seeps from my pores shows up
on my face sets up shop hangs out glares and spits
like I could not possibly be thinking
so I must be pissed
ignoring my jovial tone
my non-threatening demeanor

are you angry are you pissed people ask

hell yes I'm angry and pissed
I'm a black gay woman in america
I'm fucking lucky to be alive
this anger keeps me aware and safe
and pissed lines my spine
not my face
especially not while I'm shopping
because the cereal aisle is just a fucked place
or writing because I'm a writer
thinking

or looking at a menu
the too many choices
the how many fucking different ways does
french toast need to exist in the world dilemma

just think about it
I mean we've been hanging out for nearly three minutes
and if I haven't pissed me off and
you haven't pissed me off why would I be pissed

people
this is my humored face
if I practice an at rest face
it's not at rest it's practiced
therefore a mask and fake
which will piss me off

no offense and don't take this personally

you do know when people say this
they are totally going to offend you
and you won't be able to do
anything except take it personally

no offense and don't take this personally but
if you want to think I am pissed because
my lack of smile and at rest face
is not up to your standards
then fuck you

Ocher

orange is my favorite color in june
when the tides are high
the sky blue ocean over my head

I lose my train of thought
forget why I am here why I wish to leave
fear of jaundice and blood
scrim on the surface of memory
and moving away

wishing for legs and the directions
they travel in
there is no stillness with feet
no shuffle in your heart

nothing rhymes with orange
or its particular shade of bright
in june

I never know what weather it will wear

it has rained all month
there is no orange
it's like drowning
all over again

Hypocrisy Suite Movement #5
Caustic in G Sharp

They never wanted to be me, or us, but want to claim
these bodies the way their ancestors did.
Different day same oppression.

They have no children for me to feed this time,
my breast a buffet of a different kind.
I am allowed to feed my own kindling
for the firing squad.

Instead they crave an existence
they would have never survived.
No cream in this black, bitter
to please their plantation taste living
life on the wrong side of the big house.

Skin too delicate for sunlight and hard work
better equipped to stand on the sidelines,
watching, aiming.

My black body an auction block still,
a different kind, but still. I get to keep my clothes
on this time, cotton-close. It is my mind
they want to own,

live vicariously through me,
through us by denying the past of a people.
Label it post like it happened only once, long ago.

When post feels like yesterday, or ten minutes ago when
another brown body unarmed, no threat,
was shot in the back
by a coward in blue, again, like last time.

Another name made history through blood spatter,
a pinch of media hype.
Another mother, her child sold away, never to return.

Another one who wears skin the same color as my son.
A life that matters to me alive and breathing. A name
no hashtag could do justice.

They don't want this, not this part, so claim ignorance
or indifference like we just made that part up to justify
that it is just
about overreaction.

Even in our upset, our outrage you are more concerned
about blaming their dead bodies for not being alive
and breathing.

Justifying tragedy, secretly taking all the credit.
Make black death another thing they gave us
out of the goodness of their hearts.
Like justice.
Like freedom.

G entrified

When she started, I thought maybe she did not hear.
Maybe she did not realize I was telling my own story.
My narrative, my who, what, why, and when
but I know she heard me, in her progressive way.

She started and I thought, maybe she did not hear.
My this is about my torn, my son, his Happy Birthday,
he is getting so big that I am worried this world
will see him as dangerous black boy, the way he is growing.

Maybe she did not realize I was telling my own story.
Maybe she misunderstood the clarity of my statement.
When she touched my back, I felt the implied familiar, her
tongue in my mouth, thinks she can tell my story better than me.

When she touched my back, I wanted to break her arm.
But that would make me the angry black woman who did not
understand she was on my side. All the boys need prayers, but
my story is not all the boys just my black boy, the way he is growing.

All the boys need prayer, she says, rubbing my back with
her unbroken arm. Her tongue in my mouth prying my story
from me, reducing my son, my fear, to all boys for her comfort.
Maybe she did not realize I was telling my own story.

I know she heard me in her progressive way, her tongue
all over my story, down my throat, while I search for
a response that will not validate what she already thinks.
My mouth cannot find the right road to travel.

Reducing my son, my fear, my story: to all boys for her comfort.
My personal GPS cannot find a response to throw in her direction,
as she drags me off course while colonizing my truth, invading
my space; touching me without my permission, her progressive

gentrification.

All over my body

She does not remember that I know the "P" in her GPS means
her privilege, will always know in what direction she is going.
Even if she has to step over the bodies of black boys, or the voice
of a black boy's mother to get there.

Learning to Swim

-1-

in the process I learned things
some hard on the muscles
some sticky sweet desperate
some camouflaged remote
none the worse for it
sitting in the dark
wondering if this body could
carry me across the room

without my anchors
I float away
no one notices

not even me

-2-

spiked tongues talk
then vanish without a trace
I could use the company
cannot remember how to ask
could be the weak in me
without anchors insecurity rises

the taste of anxiety burns my throat

-3-

early in the morning
when it is still dark
sweat pools
could be tears

in the dark no one notices
not even me
when the sun greets
there is no evidence
what might have changed things
a stronger truth
a little more faith
when my train went off the tracks
the wreckage of me broadcast
on static channels

no reception between the scrawl

-4-

after the talk
after the voices screaming in my head
reduce to whispers
I sip sweet tea soaked in whiskey
look over my shoulder
in hopes of glimpsing the others who left
there is no one
I should be surprised
but nothing surprises

not any more

-5-

the birds keep on singing
the vacant smile I wear
to hide what is hidden falters
no one notices

not even me

if I come back from where I have gone

will it be noticed
will I notice the return
of my parts
things never happen in a straight line
some happen dark as dried blood

you can never deny
what has never been said

Alright—I'll call you back

when she speaks
there are times when I do not hear
the chime of her cadence
falls on ears
that cannot hear what she is not saying
I do not know what to believe
sifting through lies puncturing
the balloon of my heart

I stumble over the loose plank of replies
strapped to my tongue
better to say nothing

let it lie
like the lie we have become

when she says tomorrow
by default I think next week
next time when I become revolving door
convenience store love
quantity no quality
unless I close my eyes real tight

she threatens
promises all she will not deliver
would not know how
if she cared to explore
convinced she has no worth

rather than fighting her for her
I have become lazy gluttonous
I consume her everywhere
for our pleasure
you are worthy

I am telling her with my body
while avoiding the conversations
that go nowhere
because this is going nowhere

we have trained each other well
how to shed skin in times of need
pretend we do not need
we are busy
uncomplicated
our whiskey-mouths
and deadlines
and meetings

she only wants to talk when I cannot
I only want to talk when she will not
this ride we have jumped in and out of
for now a decade or more
familiar this carousel
this little war
of want and lust and something else
we are too shell-shocked to name

what we have become
what we have crafted
swapping horses for harnesses
as we pretend we are not dancing
to an antiquated tune
a song neither of us picked
it picked us
because we picked each other

I will bitch about this
because it is something to do
when she is not here
and I cannot make love to her

my mind travels back and forth
up and down we round the boards
always traveling in circles
vultures scavenging from one another
always ending up where we started
always shocked at how we got here

she calls
my response to every message she leaves
every siren song
is to crash on her shore

Alright—feeling the want creep in—
I call her back

Semaphore

When first we met you were a foreign concept.

I did not know if you were showing me my future,
only knew that I could not take my eyes away.

The sideways smiles offered in my direction became
a safe space, a thing I could hold on to.

I never thought you might reject the warmth of me.

Push me back into the closet I escaped years ago.
Your mouth my new favorite place.

The way you cared in that non-committal way
always reminding me that I was temporary.

In this smoky bar full of voices, vices, bad poetry
and questionable choices I approached you first.
Shared my real name, figured if you knew me I could
know you.

The purple smear along the edges of the lies you
pretended were true appealed to me in the early days.

It was a color I could relate to,
the same shade of bruises and rot.

Too sweet to be trusted as the real thing,
you artificially flavor me
into complacency.
It was delicious there.
You loved the feel of my bones under your shoes,

so convenient,
so small, the perfect resting place
for feet as busy as yours.

The lies amplify, bounce around the room.
Those off key gospel tunes do not hold
the hope they used to
no matter how many arms or flags I wave.

These days
I sleep on threadbare blankets
full of false promises
as deadly as any disease.

My only gift from you.

On Being Dipped in Water

my achilles heel
has a head full of flames
skin warm to the touch
two big eyes that see
everything
except what is right in front of them

she has a nose
that breathes in rejection
exhales misnomers
wrapped in false hopes
her mouth so full of lies
she believes they are the truth

she has a chin
it juts and struts
peahen to my cocky
shoulders with so many chips
on them the foundation
is doomed to collapse
her albatross arms stretch
squeeze so tight I wake choking
on past mistakes

her heartbeat fueled by

"what ifs"

and if the beat turns

"what if not"

no blood will flow to her lips

I have seen it before
tried to kiss her back to life with
my blood
my breath

her back holds
the weight of me
in the throws of
gymnastics passion
bouncing off every wall
and the ceiling

she turns willow
when forced to accept certain realities

she has legs that open for me

accepting the prosthetics of me
as she wraps around my waist
hips bucking for my attention

her two feet
walk in opposite directions
following a future
that can never be seen
with her two unfocused eyes

unaware that she
will never get where
she wants to be going
especially
wearing those shoes

Libation

we are all uncomfortable
I think
hands at my sides
her raw face the color of meat
downcast eyes
land on my shoes
an apology of sorts

but not really

she is concerned only
with fault lines
breaks in conversation
the kitchen is too hot
but she cannot leave
if she leaves
she admits
that this place has no room for her voice

this cannot happen

she fills it
the room
with her presence
her face full of tears
I do not hasten to assist
do not wave my white flag
surrender to her needs
she is a confused mass
of mollified hysteria
turning up the volume
of her heaving

tears will come soon

this is the part
where I am supposed to shelf myself
make all of me
all about her
who cannot handle being sidelined
becoming footnote
needs to be the life of the party
the center of the room
a conversation starter of topics
she can easily expert
easily control

like the rest of us

I do not aid in her coup
I do not make it easy
I hold my cup out in front of me
pretend to catch her reign of tears
take a healthy gulp of her sadness
her struggle
drink it all in
say AHHHHH

I can feel the change in her posture
the sharp intake of breath
the insult the agony
I continue talking about the hard truths
nobody wants to talk about
which is why the conversation keeps coming up
we are all uncomfortable
with cup in hands
swirling the dregs of her tears
the tears she uses to drown my voice
to drown my black
the sorrow she keeps close

just for this occasion

After This We Go Dark

he died
disconnected from tubes
machines
too much noise
in that room
too small to hold all the grief
all the empty lungs
too full eyes
all the drowning waiting to happen
in that room

when he died
we were ragdolls on cliffs
the precipice clawing at our feet
wanting to feel the slide and crash of us
in that too-small room
full of noise and machines
and tears up to our knees

that time he died,
I opened my mouth
an ocean fell out
washed me away
maybe
and still here in this room
there is so much noise
so much

I cannot think it all the way through
he was here and then he was gone
he was lecture and logic then massive stroke
he is the glue
now we are all sticky and confused without him

that time he died
she asked me
I was drowning right in front of her
she too much doctor to notice
again
she asked what now
I answered not knowing this would break me
in a way drowning never did
after this I would never be the same
she asked and I did not know
this would be litmus
for every relationship that follows

that time he died
she asked
I answered
point of no return
like
not ever
I do not regret this part
the not knowing the ramifications part
the lapses in and out of the dark
I only knew he would not be settled
with the odds given

after he died
these days
I am rarely settled
I am left with loving who he was
not who he is in that too loud room
unconscious while vultures circle
his organs
while lives buckle under the weight
of decisions to be made
of abandonment
of loss

he died
but I am the one
always waiting for the leaving
prepared for someone I love
not to stay

A*cknowledgments*

The poems "Amnesia" and "Ten" appear in *The Malpaís Review* Vol. 5 No.4 Spring 2015

The poem "Basa" (Hindi for bus) was prompted by the gang rape of a woman in India who was raped while the driver drove and passengers entered and exited. They raped her with a metal rod as well. She died of her injuries. Months later a football team raped a 16-year-old girl in multiple locations and she was accused in the media of ruining the football players' futures.

I have a lot of folks to thank, and I know if I start listing names I'm going to leave someone out and they will be hurt so I'm just going to say I love everybody, mostly. I want to thank my family for their constant support. My children Imani, Tia, and Zion are amazing and inspire me every day to grow up and be like them. My mother, Alice Lovelace, whose pride and support grows daily. (She can also edit the hell out of a poem.) Thanks to my amazing poetry community who listens and gives great feedback. I have had a rough time this last year, and the crew (Nate, Tawny, Anisa, Amanda, and Jordan) have kept me from nights of crippling sadness without knowing they were saving my life on countless occasions, often as a group and sometimes individually. Porch talks with Ken J, Karen, and Amy kept the ideas flowing.

Thanks friends.

About the Poet

Theresa Davis is the mother of three and was a classroom teacher for over twenty years. She reclaimed her love for poetry after the loss of her father and emerged as a nationally recognized slam poet, youth advocate, and teacher of poetry. Theresa co-founded the Art Amok Slam Team and has competed in multiple national and regional competitions culminating in 2011 when she took first place in the Women of the World Poetry Slam Competition. In recognition of her years of activism on behalf of Atlanta's youth, she was honored by the City of Atlanta with a proclamation declaring May 22, "Theresa Davis Day." In July 2012, in partnership with the City of Atlanta's Bureau of Cultural Affairs, Theresa released a chapbook, *Simon Says*—poems about teaching with anti-bullying themes. The same year, Theresa was named the 2012 McEver Chair in Poetry at Georgia Tech University, which allowed her "to reach into the community with a program of poetry events and workshops designed to recognize poetry for its possibilities and to recognize those involved in the craft of writing poetry—whether accomplished, rising, or beginning—for the artists they are." In May 2013, her first full collection of poems, *After This We Go Dark*, was published by Sibling Rivalry Press and was honored by the American Library Association through inclusion on its "Over the Rainbow" list of recommended LGBT reading, which placed the book with libraries around the world. Theresa spent most of 2014 touring with Shyla Hardwick on "The Huemyn Tour." She was featured as the opening performance poet for the band Rising Appalachia for their 2014/2015 national tour. For more information about Theresa, visit her website at http://balance2b.wix.com/theresadavis.

About the Artist

Using the carefully tooled pen, Cindy Taylor is a draughtsman in every sense of the word. She draws what she calls maps: multidimensional landscapes of unique imagery in a provocative portrayal of futuristic mythological folklore. Cindy was born and raised in New York City and now resides in Atlanta, Georgia, where she is an art teacher. She began her studies at Parson's School of Design in New York and earned her BFA from Savannah College of Art and Design. She received her graduate degree in art education from Georgia State University. For more information visit xindie.wix.com/cindytaylor.

About the Press

Sibling Rivalry Press is an independent press based in Little Rock, Arkansas. It is a sponsored project of Fractured Atlas, a nonprofit arts service organization. Contributions to support the operations of Sibling Rivalry Press are tax-deductible to the extent permitted by law, and your donations will directly assist in the publication of work that disturbs and enraptures. To contribute to the publication of more books like this one, please visit our website and click *donate*.

CPSIA information can be obtained
at www.ICGtesting.com
Printed in the USA
LVOW10s1613030717
540217LV00016B/1613/P